Seals
For Kids

Amazing Animal Books
For Young Readers

By
Rachel Smith

Mendon Cottage Books

Mendon Cottage Books
JD-Biz Corp Publishing

Read More Amazing Animal Books

Purchase at Amazon.com

Table of Contents

Introduction

Seals are a big part of several cultures throughout the world. In ancient times in Greece, they were on early coins. The Celts (people who settled in Ireland and Britain) believed that there were creatures called selkies that were like mermaids, except they hid their human sides under a seal skin.

The Inuit people, among other people, have depended on seals for a long time, and some of their legends have seals in them, including the goddess Sedna.She has a half-seal body, appearing rather like a mermaid.

Seals are spread throughout many regions of the world; they have provided humans with food, and kept other species from getting too large in numbers. They are fascinating creatures that split their time between the land and the sea.

What is a seal?

A seal is a pinniped. This refers to all kinds of seals, from the tiny Baikal seal to the enormous walrus. Pinniped means "wing-foot," which refers to the seal's fins. Instead of hands or feet, the seal has fins. This makes them not very fast on land, but in the water they can swim very fast.

A leopard seal resting on the ice.

Pinnipeds, or seals, are grouped in three families: Otariidae, (which includes sea lions and other eared seals), Odobenidae (which only includes the walrus currently), and Phocidae (which includes earless seals).

While Phocidae are considered the 'true seals,' all of the animals in these families are considered seals as well.

Seals are animals that hunt and live in the water, but tend to do other things on land. They are not nearly so mobile on land, but beware of the enormous walrus and elephant seal: they are much heavier than any human, and can hurt someone easily.

Seals spend their lives in the water. The only reasons they come on land is to escape from predators, mate, give birth, or molt. They need to breathe oxygen, and they don't have gills; instead, seals come to the surface to breathe.

Seals tend to live in more cold waters, though this isn't true of all of them. The way they're able to stay warm in such chilly temperatures is through their layer of fat. Seals are very pudgy, and it keeps them quite warm.

They are carnivores, meaning they eat other creatures. Most often, this means fish, but seals like the leopard seal will eat other creatures too, such as penguins. Walruses, despite being some of the largest seals, eat molluscs (small shelled creatures) from the bottom of the ocean.

However, seals are not at the top of the food chain. Orcas, also known as killer whales, actively hunt seals, and sharks will also hunt them.

Seals have streamlined bodies, meaning that they are designed to move through water very fast. Their four flippers (which they have instead of hands or feet) help them do this. They are not as fast as dolphins, but they are more flexible.

They also have small tails and flexible necks. Seals are also known to have fewer teeth than other carnivores. They can also retract (pull in) mammary glands, which are what they use to feed their babies, and their genitals (or private parts).

A lot of species of seals have sexual dimorphism, which means that seals of different sexes (male or female) look different. It often means that males are larger and females are smaller, though there can be a different in coloring too.

Many seals which have fur go through molting, meaning they shed the old coat of fur and grow a new one. This is something they do on land, as mentioned before.

Seals have excellent hearing and sight, designed for both the water and the land. Their elbow and ankle joints are also inside their bodies, which is how they are able to move in the water as fluidly as they can.

They also do not go to shore to sleep. Seals sleep for minutes at a time, bobbing up and down in the water. Like most marine animals, they don't go completely to sleep. Instead, only half their brain sleeps at a time, so they can notice predators and escape if they have to.

Seals also have unique lungs. When they want to dive, they force out half the air in them, and flatten their lungs. They have flattened hearts too, to allow for deflating their lungs. When a seal deflates its lungs, it closes off its nose and ears too, as well as the trachea, which is the opening in the throat that leads to the lungs. They also have ears adapted to be able to withstand the depths.

What kinds of seals are there?

There are many kinds of seals. As mentioned before, there are three families (Otariidae, Odobenidae, and Phocidae).

A bunch of Baikal seals, one of the smallest kinds of seals.

Otariidae is distinct from the other two by the fact that it mostly contains sea lions. Sea lions are more able to move around on land because their fins function more like feet than other seals' fins do. They also have ears, or ear flaps.

Odobenidae used to include a number of prehistoric creatures. They were all fairly large, but nowadays it includes only the walrus.

Walruses are distinct from the other two families due to their huge tusks.

Phocidae often have to move around on their bellies on land. They are the 'true seals' and fit a certain type. They are earless, meaning that they have no ear flaps; they can still hear quite well.

These are the three kinds, and there are many more besides.

Where did seals come from?

Seals are said to be descended from some very ancient animals indeed. However, it depends on which of the three types they are.

Australian sea lions sleeping.

One theory is that the families Otariidae and Odobenidae come from the same ancestor as bears do. There seems to be a link to land animals with seals. The other family, Phocidae, is said to come from a different animal entirely in this theory.

However, others think that all the families came from a common ancestor, perhaps an otter-like creature that originally lived in fresh water instead of salt water.

Other ancestors of the seal seem to have developed their fore flippers and hind flippers millions of years ago, gradually gaining their ability to stay out at sea as the many years passed.

The history of seals and humans

Seals have long been an important part of different human cultures. There is at least one goddess based on the seal, and many tales of seals and seal-based creatures. Also, the seal has been an important source of food for people who live in places like the Arctic and near the Arctic.

A baby harp seal.

One tale is the goddess Sedna, who is an Inuit goddess. In her tale, she got her fingers cut off and was thrown overboard off a kayak. However, in the tale, her fingers became marine animals, and she became a half-seal woman. In the tale, it is thanks to her that the Inuit have food to hunt.

Selkies have also long been a popular mythical creature among Northern-dwelling Europeans. The myth goes that there are human-like girls who hide under their sea skins. Sometimes, they will take off their seal skins, leave them on the shore, and play as humans. It's said that whoever can capture her seal skin can get her to do whatever they want. Typically, the tales involve a man taking the skin and forcing her to marry him.

But seals are not always mysterious. In places such as Northern Canada, Greenland, and other places there isn't a lot of warm land for growing things, the seal has been something of a life source for the people who live there.

Inuit peoples have lived off the seal and other creatures for centuries. They use the skins for clothes, the fat (known as blubber) for fuel and cooking, and they eat the meat. This type of people is now a target for anger because they use clubs to kill seals, even baby ones. However, it's what they have done for centuries, and they have little other options in their frozen environment for food. The same goes for whales, but that is a whole different matter.

In the world today, many zoos and marine parks keep seals as part of their attractions. Seals have been kept by zoos of sorts since about the

1600s, and they continue to be popular with people. You can find them in captivity all over the world.

Some of them are trained to do tricks. Seals have proven themselves to be fairly intelligent, able to learn such tricks and do simple experiements, such as identifying symmetry (matching things).

Some people are very upset at having seals do tricks or live in zoos. They say that it's bad for the animal, because seals are migratory and the tanks that are kept for them could never be as big as they need it to be.

Other people think it's good fun, and that the seals have adapted well to a new environment. Very few zoos or parks are intentionally cruel to their seals; a lot of work is done to keep them happy, with new ideas and studies coming out every year.

Walruses

The Walrus is in its own family, and is one of the biggest kinds of seals around. It is a strange-looking animal, with its big tusks and vibrissae.

A walrus on the beach.

The tusks are canines that are made to grow very long; they really are a type of teeth. They can grow up to a meter long, and both males and females have them.

Vibrissae are like whiskers on a mouse, but instead they detect things through the water. Walruses have some of the more sensitive vibrissae, since they need to look through the mud to find mollusks.

Walruses were hunted a lot during the past couple of centuries or so; while they had always been hunted by the native peoples in Arctic areas, there was a whole business of catching walruses and using them for their parts. This severely affected how many walruses were in the wild.

However, since humanity realized that the walruses would go extinct if they continued hunting them at that rate, the walruses rebounded a bit.

Walruses live in the northern hemisphere, near the Arctic. A lot of their time is spent on the sea ice, looking for food. And a walrus needs as much food as it can get: it can grow to be over 4,000 pounds! However, female walruses tend to only grow to about two-thirds the size of the male walrus.

There are three types of walrus: one lives in the Pacific ocean, one lives in the Leptov sea, and the last one lives in the Atlantic ocean.

The walrus starts out fairly deep brown, but slowly becomes more of a cinnamon color as time goes on and it grows up. Sometimes, males even become a sort of light pink in old age.

Most walruses have very few teeth; up to 38 can occur, but they tend to have half that or less. The way they search for food is by dragging their mouths through the sediment on the bottom of the ocean, using the vibrissae to pick up life forms and their mouths to pick them up and eat them. Tusks are not used for digging for food.

Female walruses' gestation period (how they are pregnant) lasts for several months longer than a human's. This is because they usually have the baby in February, and conditions are not good until about the time they typically have their babies. Some say it's an evolutionary adaptation.

Baby walruses are born around 100-150 pounds, and they are instantly able to swim. A mother walrus will keep the baby nursing for about a year, but the calf may end up staying with her for longer. Some have even stayed up to five years with their mother.

Walruses also migrate, taking a long trip from rocky shore or icy shore to another. There are typically tens of thousands of them together in these instances, partly because walruses are very social creatures.

The walrus can eat many kinds of food: shrimp, crabs, soft coral, and many things. However, its favorite is the clam, and other mollusks similar to it.

It also seems that they eat parts of other seals, but it's a matter of debate whether other seals are part of its normal diet.

Walruses have only two natural predators: the orca (or killer whale), and the polar bear.

Polar bear versus walrus fights are quite long-lasting affairs, when it's a fight between an adult on both sides. For this reason, polar bears don't generally attack healthy adults. Instead, they tend to try to pick off young or weak walruses. They do this two ways: one is to come running at a big group of walruses, and eat whoever gets trampled or left behind. The other is to take on an isolated walrus on land or ice. The polar bear has a big disadvantage in water; despite being able to swim, a walrus is better adapted to the water, and can seriously hurt or even kill the polar bear.

Orcas are also a threat to walruses. They tend to take on one walrus, though walruses have been known to seriously injure or fight off orcas. However, a lot of the time, the walrus will lose and be eaten.

Neither of these animals rely on walruses as their food source, which is good for them because walruses are simly not easy to bring down.

Elephant Seals

There are two types of elephant seals: Southern and Northern. They are the largest seals in the world, and especially the largest earless seal. They can get even bigger than walruses; the name 'elephant' is a very good name for them.

Elephant seals on a beach.

Elephant seals are not just named for their size, though. They're also named for the male's proboscis, a thing that looks a bit like an elephant's trunk on their face. This proboscis is used to make very loud calls to attract mates, and also to 'rebreathe,' which means reabsorbing the water that is being breathed out in normal air.

Like most seals, the elephant seal is protected from the cold by a thick layer of blubber. They are also surprisingly fast on land, as well as very heavy. But the water is their domain; they are incredibly fast swimmers and deep divers. They can hold their breath underwater for more than one and a half hours.

Elephant seals have a large amount of blood in their system, which is what allows them to stay underwater for so long. There is enough oxygen stored in their blood that they can stay down for as long as mentioned, though more often it's more like twenty to forty minutes that they spend underwater.

This type of seal bobs in the water when it sleeps; it spends most of its life in the water.

However, there is a time in the elephants seal's life that they spend on shore: when they're molting. This means they lose their fur and quite a bit of skin. They can't survive in the water like this, so they stay in a safe space called a haul out. Bulls and young adults stay in one time, and females and not near grown up elephant seals stay in another time.

They tend to eat octopuses, sharks, rays, squids, and eels, among other things.

Elephant seals live a long time, but the females are more likely to live almost twice as long as the males. It's not certain why this is, but it has proven often to be true.

Way back in the 19th century (the 1800s), this type of seal was hunted until it was almost extinct. However, now they are doing all right. The elephant seal is protected in the United States by law, and harassing, hunting, or otherwise bothering elephant seals is punishable.

The Northern elephant seal is the smaller of the two kinds. Southern elephant seals are the ones who have made the biggest records.

Sea lions

Sea lions are distinct from other seals in the fact that they can walk on all fours. They are highly intelligent creatures, and are easily trainable.

A California sea lion.

Sea lions are eared seals, meaning they have visible ear flaps. There are many kinds throughout the world, but one of the most well known is the California sea lion. It has been trained to do tricks for crowds, as well as being trained by the United States Navy. Sea lions are trained to stop unlawful scuba divers from sneaking into the country.

Also, sea lions have short, thick fur, and can weigh over 600 pounds. Not something you'd want to tangle with in the water or on land! However, attacks on humans by sea lions are incredibly rare, even in areas where sea lions and humans intermingle, such as on the beach.

There is one kind of sea lion that is extinct: the Japanese sea lion. It's said that it went extinct in the 1970's. It's a bit of a sad story; back in 1900, Japanese fisherman started going overboard in hunting the sea lions, taking in thousands. By 1915, they only took in around 300, and by later on, there were only a few dozen in the wild. Some say that the submarine warfare going on in World War II helped finish them off.

The Japanese sea lion was not even captured as food. Instead, it was valuable for its oil (blubber), its skin (leather), its whiskers, and its internal organs (medicine). A lot of them were also captured for use in circuses around this time.

They once lived in between Japan and Korea; now there are proposals to try to bring them back, or at least bring back California sea lions, who are fairly similar.

Fur Seals

Fur seals are the other eared seals. They live mostly down near the South Pole, but there are a number up around Western-most America (Alaska) and Eastern-most Russia.

A pair of South American fur seals.

Fur seals are not one group in the sense that sea lions are. Instead, they are nine groups of seals that have some things in common.

They have fur, more so than some other seals; a lot of the time, males are up to five times the size of the female. Fur seals can move their rear flippers forward like sea lions, and are well known for their speed.

Their fur has always been considered valuable, and back in older times (a hundred or so years ago), they were hunted a bit too well. Men from America, for example, would club them to death when they were in assemblages on the beach. Then they'd sell the skins in China.

Nowadays, fortunately, they are protected by various groups and laws. Very few can be hunted for anything but subsistence (to live off of). This means that the fur seal has made something of a comeback, and is doing pretty well for the most part.

They eat medium sized foods, since they're smaller than their cousins the sea lion. This includes squid and fish, and also birds. Sometimes, they are the prey of sea lions.

Conclusion

Seals are a fascinating group with many different creatures in them. From the enormous elephant seal to the tiny Baikal seal, it is good for the environment for them to be there. Without them there to both be predator and pray, our ecosystem would have trouble.

That's why humans don't hunt seals to the extent that they used to. We're on a path to better environments for animals like seals, and hopefully, we will stay on that path.

Author Bio

Rachel Smith is a young author who enjoys animals. Once, she had a rabbit who was very nervous, and chewed through her leash and tried to escape. She had pet fish, including a pink kissing gourami that liked to eat the other fish. She's also had several pet mice, who were the funniest little animals to watch. She lives in Ohio with her family and writes in her spare time.

Our books are available at
1. Amazon.com

2. Barnes and Noble

3. Itunes

4. Kobo

5. Smashwords

6. Google Play Books

Publisher

JD-Biz Corp

P O Box 374

Mendon, Utah 84325

http://www.jd-biz.com/

Made in the USA
Middletown, DE
17 June 2023

32760977R00020